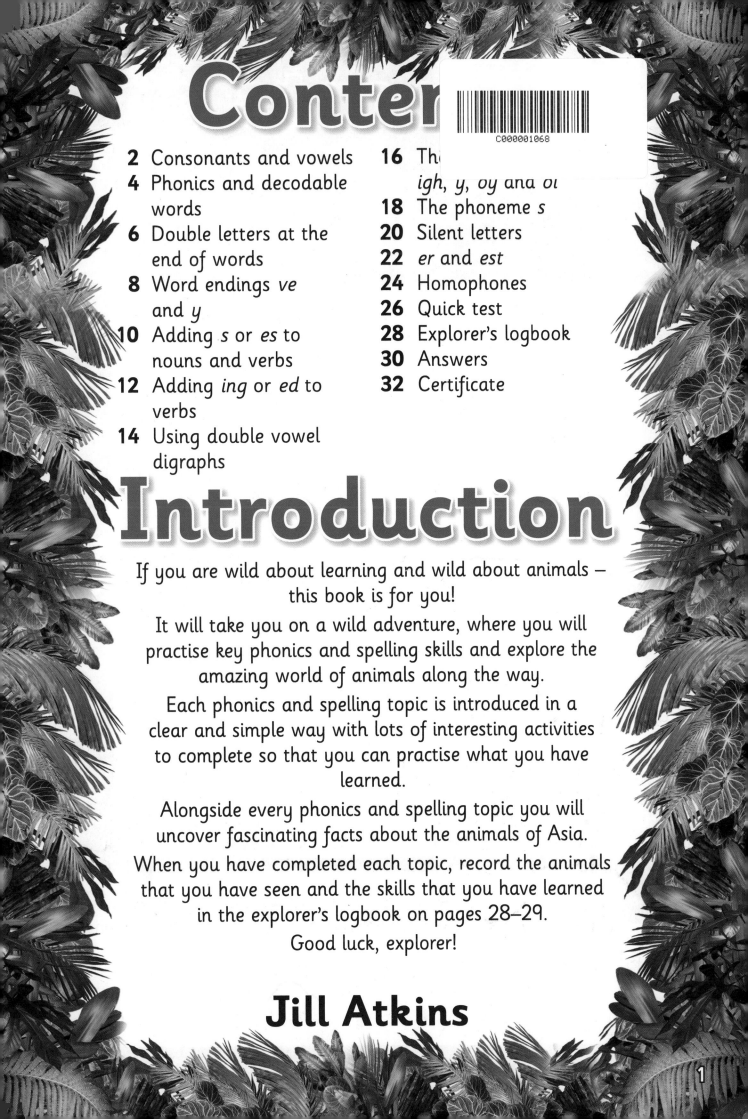

Contents

2 Consonants and vowels

4 Phonics and decodable words

6 Double letters at the end of words

8 Word endings *ve* and *y*

10 Adding *s* or *es* to nouns and verbs

12 Adding *ing* or *ed* to verbs

14 Using double vowel digraphs

16 Th... *igh*, *y*, *oy* and *o...*

18 The phoneme *s*

20 Silent letters

22 *er* and *est*

24 Homophones

26 Quick test

28 Explorer's logbook

30 Answers

32 Certificate

Introduction

If you are wild about learning and wild about animals – this book is for you!

It will take you on a wild adventure, where you will practise key phonics and spelling skills and explore the amazing world of animals along the way.

Each phonics and spelling topic is introduced in a clear and simple way with lots of interesting activities to complete so that you can practise what you have learned.

Alongside every phonics and spelling topic you will uncover fascinating facts about the animals of Asia.

When you have completed each topic, record the animals that you have seen and the skills that you have learned in the explorer's logbook on pages 28–29.

Good luck, explorer!

Jill Atkins

Consonants and vowels

Words are made up of letters called **consonants** and **vowels**.

Most of the letters in the alphabet are consonants: **b, c, d, f, g, h, j, k, l, m, n, p, q,** r, s, t, v, w, x, y, z.

When two consonants come together, they make a **digraph** if they make a single sound.

For example:

ch *chop*   **sh** *shoe*   **ll** *sill*

If two consonants come together and each consonant makes its own sound, they make a **consonant blend**.

For example:

st *list*   **fl** *flop*   **gr** *grip*

There are five vowels: **a, e, i, o, u**.

Most words have at least one vowel. Some words begin with a vowel: *elephant* begins with a vowel.

Some words have more than one vowel.
For example, there are three vowels in *elephant*: **e, e, a**.

Task 1

Write one vowel in the gap in each of these simple words. Now read the word. Some have more than one possible answer.

a f_o_x   c k_u_d   e c_a_n   g y_e_s   i w_i_t

b t_u_b   d l_i_d   f r_u_g   h j_i_m   j z_a_p

Task 2

Put a vowel into each gap to make a word with a consonant blend or a digraph at the beginning.

a ch_a_p   g dr_a_g

b fl_a_t   h sh_e_d

c sp__n   i pl_a_n

d gr_a_b   j th__t

e sw_i_m   k sl_a_t

f tr_u_p   l tr__m

Task 3

Put a vowel into each gap to make a word with a consonant blend or a digraph at the end.

a l__ts   e b_a_nd   i g__ft

b m__ch   f c_a_mp   j b__lb

c s_a_ng   g w_a_nt   k l__nk

d d_o_ck   h v_e_st   l k__pt

WILD FACT

Elephants live in strong family groups. They protect their young, called calves, from predators.

Task 4

Add vowels into these longer words. They are in sentences to help you.

a The **d__nt__st** looks after your teeth.

b The **r__ck__t** went up to the moon.

c A **r__b__n** is a bird that lives in the garden.

d At Halloween we use a **p__mpk__n** to make a lantern.

Now swing your trunk and lumber to pages 28–29 to record what you have learned in your explorer's logbook.

Phonics and decodable words

Animal: Silkworm
I live in: Mulberry trees around the world
I eat: Mulberry leaves
I weigh: Less than 1 g

Words are made up of consonants, vowels, digraphs and trigraphs put together.

Trigraphs are when three letters are put together to make one sound, for example, **tch** as in *stitch* and **dge** as in *hedge*.

Here are some of the words from the wild facts about the silkworm. They all have a consonant blend.

stop   *just*   *spin*   *silk*

You can split words to make them easier to read:

st-op   ju-st   sp-in   si-lk

WILD FACT

The silkworm spins 900 metres of silk fibre in just 3 days to make a cocoon around itself. The silk is woven into cloth to make clothes.

Task 1   Draw lines to join word beginnings with word ends to make whole words.

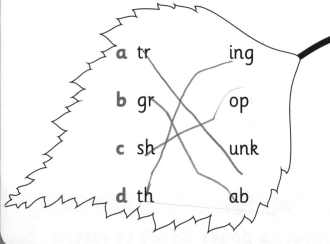

a tr   ing

b gr   op

c sh   unk

d th   ab

Task 2 Some of these words are made up and do not make sense! Circle the real words.

a (take) jom (flop) (bake) shiz

b blemp (jam) pline (week) (twin)

c (soggy) dack (flow) teeb hoob

d doy (chop) (kill) (silk) jall

Task 3 Make up your own nonsense words by using the beginning of one real word and the ending of another.

a _~~boob~~_

b _diveonboo_

c _away_

WILD FACT

The silkworm is a caterpillar. As soon as it hatches, it eats mulberry leaves non-stop for 35 days!

Task 4 The table shows words with consonant blends, digraphs and trigraphs. Put a tick in one box for each row to show which each word has. The first one has been done for you:

	Consonant blend	Digraph	Trigraph
such		✓	
catch		✓	✓
stay	✓		
hedge			✓
shut		✓	
duck		✓	

Now wriggle along to pages 28–29 to record what you have learned in your explorer's logbook.

Double letters at the end of words

FACT FILE

Animal: Green peafowl

I live in: Forests of India, Pakistan and Sri Lanka

I eat: Seeds, fruit, plants and small mammals

I weigh: 5 kg

When the sounds **f**, **s**, **z** and **l** are at the end of a word, they are doubled: **ff**, **ss**, **zz**, **ll**, for example, in the words *stiff*, *cross*, *fizz* and *ball*.

Some words have **c** and **k** at the end. Together they make the sound **k**. For example, *trick*.

Task 1 Explore the Wild Facts and discover two words that end with 'ck'. Write them on the lines.

peacock

black peachick

Task 2 Add **ck** to each of these words and read them.

a thick   **d** peck   **g** muck

b black   **e** shock   **h** quack

c sock   **f** flick

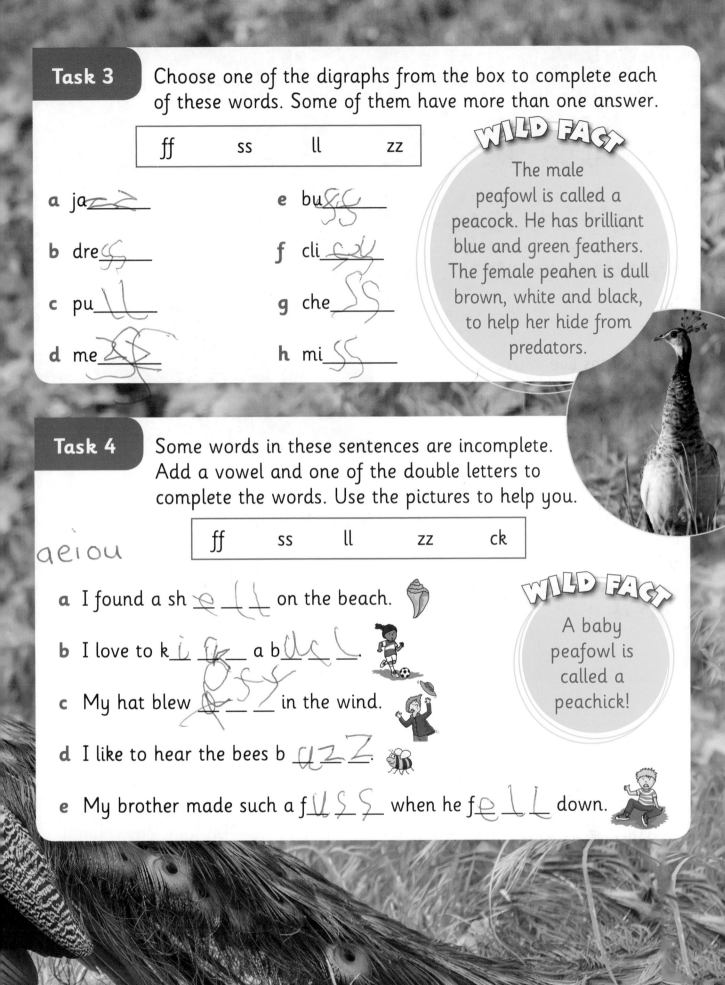

Task 3 Choose one of the digraphs from the box to complete each of these words. Some of them have more than one answer.

| ff | ss | ll | zz |

a ja__zz__

b dre__ss__

c pu__ll__

d me__ss__

e bu__ss__

f cli__ff__

g che__ss__

h mi__ss__

WILD FACT

The male peafowl is called a peacock. He has brilliant blue and green feathers. The female peahen is dull brown, white and black, to help her hide from predators.

Task 4 Some words in these sentences are incomplete. Add a vowel and one of the double letters to complete the words. Use the pictures to help you.

aeiou

| ff | ss | ll | zz | ck |

a I found a sh__e ll__ on the beach.

b I love to k__i ck__ a b__a ll__.

c My hat blew __o ff__ in the wind.

d I like to hear the bees b__uzz__.

e My brother made such a f__uss__ when he f__ell__ down.

WILD FACT

A baby peafowl is called a peachick!

Now strut along to pages 28–29 to record what you have learned in your explorer's logbook.

Word endings ve and y

Sometimes words end in unexpected ways.

Orangutans live in trees.

There is a **v** sound at the end of *live* as the **e** is silent.

There are different ways of pronouncing a **y** when it comes at the end of a word. It can sound like **ee** as in *happy*, but it can also sound like **eye** as in *fly*.

FACT FILE

Animal: Orangutan
I live in: Trees in the forests of Southeast Asia
I eat: Fruit, plants, insects, small birds and animals
I weigh: 50 kg

Task 1

Choose one of the words from the box to fill each of the gaps.

have	twelve	love	sleeve	shave	wave

a My dad has a ~~shave~~ every day.

b I ~~love~~ watching the orangutans play.

c When I go home, I ~~wave~~ goodbye to my friends.

d My arm slides into my ~~sleeve~~.

e There are ~~twelve~~ eggs in the box.

f I ~~have~~ a drink of milk before I go to bed.

WILD FACT

The orangutan walks on four legs when it is on the ground, but in the trees it swings from branch to branch using its arms.

Task 2   Write two words that rhyme with the word at the beginning of each line.

a **save** _wave cave_

b **five** _give live_

c **love** _above glove_

d **give** _live live_

e **leave** _pease keas_
believe receive

Task 3   Read the words in the box then put them into the correct group. The first two have been done for you.

| try | very | fly | spy | merry | fairy | cry | fry | happy |
| why | shy | puppy | silly | candy | my | windy | mummy | by |

Words with a 'y' ending that sounds like 'eye'	Words with a 'y' ending that sounds like 'ee'
try	very
fly	fairy
spy	puppy
shy	merry
why	candy
my	silly
cry	windy
fry	happy
by	mummy

Now swing along to pages 28–29 to record what you have learned in your explorer's logbook.

Adding s or es to nouns and verbs

A noun is a person, place, or thing. To make many nouns plural (more than one person, place or thing), you can just add **s**, but some nouns ending with certain letters need **es**.

Make a plural with **s**: nouns ending in **a**, **b**, **d**, **e**, **f**, **ff**, **g**, **gg**, **ck**, **l**, **ll**, **m**, **n**, **p**, **r**, **t**, **w**.

For example: *bats*, *chicks*, *eggs*

Make a plural with **es**: nouns ending in **s**, **ss**, **x**, **zz**, **ch**, **tch**, **sh**.

For example: *boxes*, *stitches*, *buzzes*

Sometimes a verb (a doing or being word) needs to be changed in the same way.

FACT FILE

Animal:	Fruit bat
I live in:	Dense forests of southern Asia
I eat:	Fruit juices and flower nectar
I weigh:	1 kg

Task 1 Make these singular nouns into plurals by adding **s** or **es**.

a cat_s_   witch_es_   banana_s_   fox_es_   buzz_es_

b dog_s_   window_s_   church_es_   chip_s_   kiss_es_

c bus_es_   toy_s_   lad_s_   cliff_es_   dish_es_

d animal_s_   duck_s_   pill_s_   cow_s_   class_es_

Task 2   Circle the correct plural for each of these nouns.

a **glass**   glasss   glasses

b **broom**   brooms   broomes

c **watch**   watches   watchs

d **six**   sixs   sixes

e **lunch**   lunches   lunchs

f **dolphin** dolphins dolphines

g **apple**   applees   apples

h **bush**   bushs   bushes

i **peg**   pegs   peges

j **truck**   trucks   truckes

WILD FACT

The fruit bat's wings are long fingers covered in thin skin.

Task 3   Fill in the missing words by adding **s** or **es** to the bold verbs in these sentences.

WILD FACT

The fruit bat is the largest of all the bats. It is sometimes called the flying fox, although it is not related to the fox.

a I **run** to see the fruit bat. Millie

_____ to see the fruit bat.

b I **show** my picture to my mum. Sam

_____ his picture to his mum.

c I **hiss** loudly. The snake _____ loudly.

d I **ring** the doorbell. Fred _____ the doorbell.

e I **fix** the lock on the box. Dad _____ the lock on the box.

f I **fill** my glass with water. Mum _____ my glass with water.

Now flap to pages 28–29 to record what you have learned in your explorer's logbook.

Adding ing or ed to verbs

Verbs are **doing** or **being** words. Sometimes you can use the simple form of the word. This is called the **root word**.

For example:

inject   climb   stay   weigh

You can add **ing** or **ed** at the end of the word to change the way each word is used, without needing to change the spelling of the word itself.

For example:

sting ⟶ stinging   climb ⟶ climbed

FACT FILE

Animal: Scorpion
I live in: Deserts, rainforests, grasslands and the seashore
I eat: Insects and small animals
I weigh: 60 g

Task 1   Add **ing** and **ed** to each of these root words. The first one has been done for you.

| **climb** | climbing | climbed |

a **inject** _____ _____

b **stay** _____ _____

c **weigh** _____ _____

Task 2

These verbs describe what a scorpion does. Add **ing** and **ed** to each of them.

a **hunt** _____ _____

b **pinch** _____ _____

c **poison** _____ _____

Task 3

Make your own list of verbs that can be changed in the same way without altering the root word.

_____

_____

Task 4

These words all end with **ng**. Add **ng** to each word and read the word.

a sa__ __

b thi__ __

c go__ __

d bri __ __

e hu__ __

f belo__ __

g ri__ __

h lu__ __

i ki__ __

j fa__ __

k ru__ __

l po__ __

Now dart to pages 28–29 to record what you have learned in your explorer's logbook.

Using double vowel digraphs

You already know that a digraph is a single sound made with two letters. The sound it makes is called a **phoneme**. A **grapheme** is the written form of that sound. For example, consonant digraphs like **ch**, **sh**, **ck**.

Sometimes, double vowels in words show a phoneme. For example, you can double **o** to make **oo**, as in *fool*. Make a circle with your lips and say that sound.

You can also use double **e** to make **ee**, as in *feet*. Now widen your mouth and say that sound.

FACT FILE

Animal:	Red panda
I live in:	The cold mountain forests of Asia
I eat:	Bamboo, fruit, flowers and eggs
I weigh:	5–9 kg

Task 1 Read this passage about the red panda. Find and write four words with the **oo** grapheme.

The red panda is much smaller than the giant panda. It has black and white markings on its face, and a striped tail like a racoon. Its favourite food is bamboo shoots and leaves.

_____   _____

_____   _____

Task 2 Complete these **oo** words. Make the second word rhyme with the first word.

a m__ __n   s__ __ __

b h__ __p   l__ __ __

c z__ __m   b__ __ __

d f__ __d   m__ __ __

Task 3 Now hunt about in the Wild Facts to find three words with the **ee** grapheme. Write them on the lines.

_____   _____   _____

Task 4 Find more words with **ee** that rhyme with these words. The first letter is given each time to help you.

a seek   w __ __ __

b peep   k __ __ __

c meet   f __ __ __

d need   w __ __ __

e feel   h __ __ __

Now scamper to pages 28–29 to record what you have learned in your explorer's logbook.

The graphemes ie, i-e, igh, y, oy and oi

Many words have graphemes that sound the same but are made up of different digraphs and trigraphs.

These digraphs and trigraphs sound the same: **ie**, **i-e**, **igh**, **y**.

In the same way, **oi** and **oy** sound the same. The **oy** digraph usually comes at the end of a word, for example, *boy*.

The digraph **oi** is usually in the middle of a word, for example, *noise*.

FACT FILE

Animal:	Saltwater crocodile
I live in:	Salt water, mangrove swamps, lakes and river estuaries
I eat:	Fish, birds and animals, including humans!
I weigh:	Up to 1,000 kg

Task 1 Write two words that rhyme with each of the words in bold.

a **boy** _____

b **coil** _____

c **join** _____

Task 2 Write a word spelled with **oi** or **oy** in these sentences.

a I have a sore throat and I have lost my v__ __ __ __.

b I like to j__ __ __ in with all the games.

c I planted a seed in the s__ __ __.

d The referee tossed a c__ __ __ to see who would start.

e I found my car in the t__ __ box.

f Stop cheating! You will s__ __ __ __ the game!

WILD FACT

Saltwater crocodiles camouflage themselves in murky water and mud. They lie in wait for their prey and then lunge forward and snap their powerful jaws together!

Task 3 Use the words in the box to complete the sentences. The first letter of each word has been given to help you.

light	tight	lie	tie	side	bite
like	kite	cry	fly	my	

WILD FACT

The saltwater crocodile is the largest of all the reptiles. It can grow to 5 metres long. It is extremely dangerous to humans.

a It was dark, so I put on the l__ __ __ __ .

b When I l__ __ in bed, I turn on my s__ __ __.

c I b__ __ __ on my apple.

d My brother upset me and made me c__ __.

e I t__ __ the string in a t__ __ __ __ knot.

f I l__ __ __ to f__ __   m__   k__ __ __.

Now snap your teeth and lunge forward to pages 28–29 to record what you have learned in your explorer's logbook.

17

The phoneme s

When a letter **c** is followed by a letter **e**, letter **i** or letter **y**, it is sounded **s**.

For example:

ce → *ice*   ci → *pencil*

cy → *fancy*

FACT FILE

Animal: Asiatic black bear
I live in: Forests, hills and mountains
I eat: Leaves, nuts, fruits, berries, eggs, insects, birds and small mammals
I weigh: 60–220 kg

WILD FACT

The Asiatic black bear has a cream, crescent-shaped marking on its chest, so it is often called the moon bear.

Task 1   Write three words that rhyme with **ace** and **ice**.

a **ace** _____   _____   _____

b **ice** _____   _____   _____

Task 2 Underline all the words in the bear where the **c** is sounded **s**.

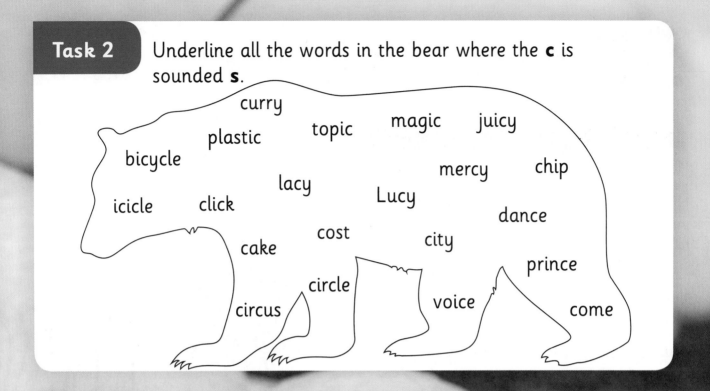

curry

plastic   topic   magic   juicy

bicycle

mercy   chip

lacy   Lucy

icicle   click

dance

cost   city

cake

prince

circle   voice   come

circus

Task 3 Fill in the crossword with words spelled with a **c** followed by **e**, **i** or **y**.

Across

2 You run to win this.

4 The rocket shoots up into this.

5 I f _ _ _ _ an ice cream.

Down

1 The country across the English Channel.

3 Sugar and s _ _ _ _ and all things nice.

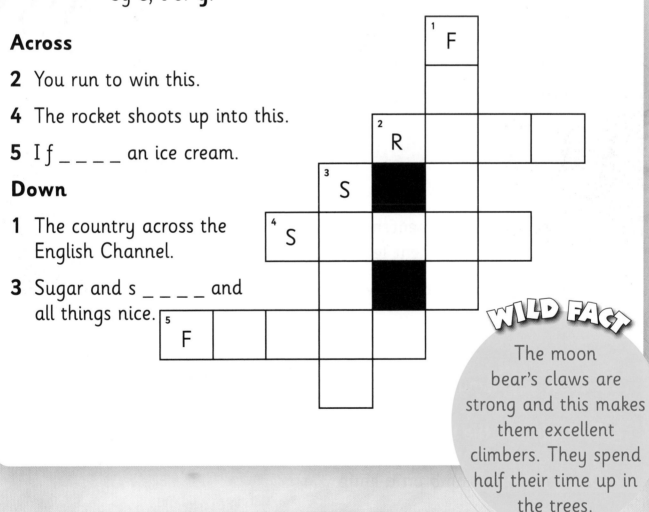

Now climb through the trees to pages 28–29 to record what you have learned in your explorer's logbook.

Silent letters

Lots of words have **silent letters**. A silent letter is a letter that cannot be heard when the word is spoken.

Here are some examples of silent letters:

u after **q** ———→ quack

k before **n** ———→ knight

w before **r** ———→ wrap

b after **m** ———→ crumb

h after **g** ———→ ghost

Sometimes, other letters are silent in a word, for example: **c, l, s, t, n**.

Task 1 Read these sentences then search for words that have silent letters. Underline them.

a My knees began to knock when I saw the tiger.

b Jack was as white as a ghost.

c I know why Amy went the wrong way.

d Tom climbed the tree quite quickly.

e Daisy cut her thumb on a knife.

f Rowan fell down and broke his wrist.

FACT FILE

Animal: Bengal tiger

I live in: Swamps, grasslands and rainforests

I eat: Wild boar, deer and many other animals, even humans

I weigh: Up to 230 kg

Task 2 Find and circle two words in each line which have a silent letter.

a gone   gnome   groan   ghost

b plum   knit   numb   slum

c knight   king   wring   kite

d gnat   grain   queen   stick

e wriggle   smart   hatch   crumb

WILD FACT

The tiger is the biggest wild cat in the world.

WILD FACT

Tigers live in areas full of trees, bushes and clumps of tall grass, where their stripes give them camouflage in among the shadows.

Task 3 Spot the word that has the silent letter and underline it.

a **silent c:**   scorch   scamp   scissors   scar

b **silent l:**   take   talk   took   trick

c **silent s:**   island   inside   igloos   illness

d **silent t:**   bitter   filter   listen   wilted

e **silent n:**   auntie   name   under   autumn

Now pad silently on to pages 28–29 to record what you have learned in your explorer's logbook.

er and est

We can describe animals and objects by using **adjectives**.

Then we can add **er** to the adjective to show it is **more than** as we described.

We can add **est** to the adjective to show that it is **the most** it could be.

For example: A _sharp_ knife A _sharper_ knife The _sharpest_ knife

If there is already an **e** at the end of the word, we just need to add **r** and **st**.

Task 1

Add **er** then **est** to each of these adjectives and then read them. The first one has been done for you.

hard   harder   hardest

a cool   _____   _____

b soft   _____   _____

c great   _____   _____

Task 2

Add **r** then **st** to each of these adjectives and then read them. The first one has been done for you.

late   later   latest

a wise   _____   _____

b simple   _____   _____

c strange   _____   _____

Task 3

When words have just one vowel in the middle and one consonant at the end, that last consonant is doubled. Double the last consonant, then add **er** then **est** to each of these adjectives and then read them. The first one has been done for you.

fat	fatter	fattest
a red	_____	_____
b sad	_____	_____
c thin	_____	_____

WILD FACT

The female Burmese python lays up to 100 eggs, which she keeps warm by wrapping herself gently round them and shivering.

Task 4

When words end in **y**, we change the **y** to an **i** before adding **er** or **est**. Change the **y** to an **i** then add **er** and **est** to each of these adjectives. Now read them. The first one has been done for you.

busy	busier (more busy)	busiest (most busy)
a silly	_____	_____
b lazy	_____	_____
c funny	_____	_____

Now slither to pages 28–29 to record what you have learned in your explorer's logbook.

Homophones

FACT FILE

Animal: Bactrian camel
I live in: Deserts and grasslands
I eat: Grass, plants, leaves and seeds
I weigh: Around 600–1,000 kg

Homophones are two or more words that sound the same but have different meanings and spellings.

Search the Wild Facts and find a word that sounds like *there* (meaning 'in that place'). Yes, you're right. It is *their* (meaning 'belonging to them').

WILD FACT

If camels feel threatened, they will spit out their really stinky spit! You can tell if a camel is about to spit: its cheeks fill up and bulge. So stand well back!

Task 1 Read the sentences below and fill in the gaps by using **there** or **their** in the right places.

a The children took __ __ __ __ __ dog for a walk.

b Look at that camel over __ __ __ __ __!

c __ __ __ __ __ __ are lots of camels in Asia.

d The dogs wagged __ __ __ __ __ tails when they saw __ __ __ __ __ master.

Task 2

Choose the correct homophone from the brackets to complete the sentence.

a I went to the shops to _____ an apple. **(buy / by)**

b I have been waiting all _____ to see a camel. **(week / weak)**

c The wind _____ the sand across the desert. **(blue / blew)**

WILD FACT

The Bactrian camel can go without water for several weeks. When it finds water, it can drink over 100 litres in one go!

Task 3

Choose the homophone from the box that makes sense to complete the sentences.

| to | too | two |

a It was much _____ hot in the desert.

b We went _____ see the camels in the zoo.

c Bactrian camels have _____ humps each.

Now stroll along to pages 28–29 to record what you have learned in your explorer's logbook.

Quick test

Now try these questions. Give yourself **1 mark** for every correct answer.

1 Add the correct endings to these adjectives so that they show **more than** and **the most** for each one.

a smart _____ _____

b easy _____ _____

c wet _____ _____

d nice _____ _____

2 Make these singular nouns into plural nouns by adding **s** or **es** at the end.

a brush   b cub   c cave

3 Write the homophone that makes sense in each sentence.

deer / dear

a There are many _____ roaming in the woods.

b You are my _____ friend.

not / knot

c I have a _____ in my shoe lace.

d A camel's spit is _____ very nice!

write / right

e I will _____ a letter to my grandma.

f I am _____-handed, but my mum is left-handed.

4 Put a vowel into each of these spaces in the words so that the sentences make sense.

a I bought a r__bb__t at the p__t sh__p.

b My d__d w__nt to the sh__ps.

c The c__p of m__lk was very h__t.

d I love f__sh and ch__ps for my d__nn__r.

5 Make **five** words out of these consonants, vowels and trigraphs.

Consonants	Vowels	Trigraphs
c w h d b	a e i o u	tch dge

_____ _____ _____

_____ _____

6 Write a rhyming word for each of these words. They must all have a silent letter. ☐

   a crumb   _____

   b life   _____

   c long   _____

   d toast   _____

   e fist   _____

7 Write **five** words where the letter **c** sounds **s**. ☐

_____   _____   _____

_____   _____

8 Complete these words using **ck**, **ff**, **ll**, **ss** or **zz**. ☐

   a bri__ __   **b** acro__ __   **c** flu__ __

   d tri__ __   **e** whi__ __   **f** dre__ __

   g hu__ __   **h** sti__ __   **i** ta__ __

9 Write a rhyming word that is also spelled with **oo** for each of these words. ☐

   a roof   _____

   b pool   _____

   c hoot   _____

10 Complete these words using **ie**, **i-e**, **igh** or **y**. Some have more than one answer. ☐

   a b_____   **b** h_____   **c** l_____

   d fl_____   **e** tr_____   **f** sh_____

11 Add **ed** or **ing** to complete the words so that the sentences make sense. ☐

   a I was go _____ to school when I met a dog.

   b The lady show _____ me the way to the park.

   c I have always want _____ a hamster.

   d The fruit bat is fly _____ in and out of the trees.

   e The scorpion dart _____ towards the rocks.

   f The python is slither _____ away.

12 Add a word ending in 'y' that rhymes with the first line in each verse. ☐

   a The croc was very happy,

      Its teeth were very _____.

   b The day was warm and sunny,

      The clown was very _____.

How did you do?   1–12 Try again!   13–25 Good try!   /50

26–37 Great work!   38–50 Excellent exploring!

Explorer's Logbook

Tick off the topics as you complete them and then colour in the star.

Consonants and vowels ☐

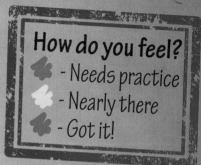

Phonics and decodable words ☐

Double letters at the end of words ☐

Word endings ve and y ☐

Adding s or es to nouns and verbs ☐

Adding *ing* or *ed* to verbs ☐

The graphemes *ie, i-e, igh, y, oy* and *oi* ☐

Using double vowel digraphs ☐

The phoneme *s* ☐

Silent letters ☐

er and *est* ☐

Homophones ☐

29

Answers

Task 1

a fox / fix   **b** tub / tab   **c** kid   **d** lid / lad / led
e can   **f** rag / rig / rug   **g** yes   **h** jam
i wet / wit   **j** zip / zap

Task 2

a chop / chip / chap   **b** flat / flit
c spin / spun / span   **d** grab / grub
e swim / swam / swum   **f** trap / trip
g drag / dreg / drug   **h** shed / shod
i plan   **j** that
k slit / slat / slot   **l** trim / tram

Task 3

a lets / lots   **b** much   **c** sing / sang / sung / song
d deck / dock / duck   **e** band / bend / bond / bind
f camp   **g** want / went   **h** vest / vast
i gift   **j** bulb   **k** link   **l** kept

Task 4

a The d**enti**st looks after your teeth.
b The r**ocke**t went up to the moon.
c A r**obi**n is a bird that lives in the garden.
d At Halloween we use a p**umpki**n to make a lantern.

Pages 4–5
Task 1

a trunk   **b** grab   **c** shop   **d** thing

Task 2

a take, flop, bake   **b** jam, week, twin
c soggy, flow   **d** chop, kill, silk

Task 3

Any combination of consonants and vowels

Task 4

	Consonant blend	Digraph	Trigraph
such		✓	
catch			✓
stay	✓		
hedge			✓
shut		✓	
duck		✓	

Pages 6–7
Task 1

Two from peacock, peachick, black

Task 2

a thick   **b** black   **c** sock   **d** peck
e shock   **f** flick   **g** muck   **h** quack

Task 3

a jazz   **b** dress   **c** pull / puff / puss
d mess   **e** bull / buzz / buff   **f** cliff
g chess   **h** mill / miss / miff

Task 4

a I found a **shell** on the beach.
b I love to **kick** a **ball**.
c My hat blew **off** in the wind.
d I like to hear the bees **buzz**.
e My brother made such a **fuss** when he **fell** down.

Pages 8–9
Task 1

a My dad has a **shave** every day.
b I **love** watching the orangutans play.
c When I go home I **wave** goodbye to my friends.
d My arm slides into my **sleeve**.
e There are **twelve** eggs in the box.
f I **have** a drink of milk before I go to bed.

Task 2

a Any rhyming word, e.g. cave, brave, Dave, crave, grave, nave, rave, slave, wave
b Any rhyming word, e.g. alive, dive, drive, hive, jive, live
c Any rhyming word, e.g. above, dove, glove
d Any rhyming word, e.g. live, sieve
e Any rhyming word, e.g. believe, grieve, heave, sleeve, Steve, weave

Task 3

Words with a 'y' ending that sounds like 'eye'	Words with a 'y' ending that sounds like 'ee'
try	very
fly	merry
spy	fairy
cry	happy
fry	puppy
why	silly
shy	candy
my	windy
by	mummy

Pages 10–11
Task 1

a cat**s**, witch**es**, banana**s**, fox**es**, buzz**es**
b dog**s**, window**s**, church**es**, chip**s**, kiss**es**
c bus**es**, toy**s**, lad**s**, cliff**s**, dish**es**
d animal**s**, duck**s**, pill**s**, cow**s**, class**es**

Task 2

a glasses   **b** brooms   **c** watches   **d** sixes
e lunches   **f** dolphins   **g** apples   **h** bushes
i pegs   **j** trucks

Task 3

a Millie **runs** to see the fruit bat.
b Sam **shows** his picture to his mum.
c The snake **hisses** loudly.
d Fred **rings** the doorbell.
e Dad **fixes** the lock on the box.
f Mum **fills** my glass with water.

Pages 12–13
Task 1

a injecting, injected
b staying, stayed
c weighing, weighed

Task 2

a hunting, hunted
b pinching, pinched
c poisoning, poisoned

Task 3

Any word that can have **ing** and **ed** added without altering the root word

Task 4

a sang   **b** thing   **c** gong   **d** bring
e hung   **f** belong   **g** ring   **h** lung
i king   **j** fang   **k** rung   **l** pong

Pages 14–15
Task 1

food, bamboo, shoots, racoon

Task 2

a moon, soon   **b** hoop, loop
c zoom, boom   **d** food, mood

Task 3

trees, sleeps, feet

Task 4

a week   **b** keep   **c** feet

d weed   **e** heel

Pages 16–17

Task 1

a Any two words that rhyme, e.g. joy, toy, enjoy, annoy

b Any two words that rhyme, e.g. oil, foil, boil, soil, toil

c Any two words that rhyme, e.g. coin, loin

Task 2

a I have a sore throat and I have lost my **voice**.

b I like to **join** in with all the games.

c I planted a seed in the **soil**.

d The referee tossed a **coin** to see who would start.

e I found my car in the **toy** box.

f Stop cheating! You will **spoil** the game!

Task 3

a It was dark, so I put on the **light**.

b When I **lie** in bed, I turn on my **side**.

c I **bite** on my apple.

d My brother upset me and made me **cry**.

e I **tie** the string in a **tight** knot.

f I **like** to **fly my kite**.

Pages 18–19

Task 1

a Any three words that rhyme, e.g. face, lace, pace, race, trace

b Any two words that rhyme, e.g. dice, lice, mice, nice, price, rice, slice, twice

Task 2

bicycle, juicy, lacy, Lucy, mercy, icicle, prince, city, voice, dance, circle, circus

Task 3

Across: 2 race, 4 space, 5 fancy, **Down:** 1 France, 3 spice

Pages 20–21

Task 1

a My knees began to knock when I saw the tiger.

b Jack was as white as a ghost.

c I know why Amy went the wrong way.

d Tom climbed the tree quite quickly.

e Daisy cut her thumb on a knife.

f Rowan fell down and broke his wrist.

Task 2

a gnome, ghost   **b** knit, numb

c knight, wring   **d** gnat, queen

e wriggle, crumb

Task 3

a scissors   **b** talk   **c** island

d listen   **e** autumn

Pages 22–23

Task 1

a cool, cooler, coolest   **b** soft, softer, softest

c great, greater, greatest

Task 2

a wise, wiser, wisest   **b** simple, simpler, simplest

c strange, stranger, strangest

Task 3

a red, redder, reddest   **b** sad, sadder, saddest

c thin, thinner, thinnest

Task 4

a silly, sillier, silliest   **b** lazy, lazier, laziest

c funny, funnier, funniest

Pages 24–25

Task 1

a The children took **their** dog for a walk.

b Look at that camel over **there!**

c **There** are lots of camels in Asia.

d The dogs wagged **their** tails when they saw **their** master.

Task 2

a I went to the shops to **buy** an apple.

b I have been waiting all **week** to see a camel.

c The wind **blew** the sand across the desert.

Task 3

a It was much **too** hot in the desert.

b We went **to** see the camels in the zoo.

c Bactrian camels have **two** humps each.

Pages 26–27

1 a smarter, smartest   **b** easier, easiest

    c wetter, wettest   **d** nicer, nicest

2 a brushes   **b** cubs   **c** caves

3 a There are many **deer** roaming in the woods.

    b You are my **dear** friend.

    c I have a **knot** in my shoe lace.

    d A camel's spit is **not** very nice!

    e I will **write** a letter to my grandma.

    f I am **right**-handed, but my mum is left-handed.

4 a I bought a ra**bb**it at the pet sh**o**p.

    b My d**a**d w**e**nt to the sh**o**ps.

    c The c**u**p of m**i**lk was very h**o**t.

    d I love **f**ish and **ch**ips for my di**nn**er.

5 Any five from: batch, botch, catch, hatch, watch, ditch, hitch, witch, hutch, badge, bodge, budge, cadge, hedge, dodge, wodge

6 a e.g. numb, thumb, dumb

    b e.g. knife

    c e.g. wrong

    d e.g. ghost

    e e.g. wrist

7 Any five words, e.g. juice, juicy, voice, nice, grace, pace, once, twice, ice, lice, icy, pencil, icicle, city, cycle, mercy, fancy, mice

8 a bri**ck**   **b** a**cross**   **c** flu**ff**

    d tri**ck** / tri**ll**   **e** whi**ff** or whi**zz**

    f dre**ss**   **g** hu**ll** / hu**ff**

    h sti**ff** / sti**ck** / sti**ll**   **i** ta**ll** / ta**ck**

9 a Any rhyming word with **oo**, e.g. hoof, goof

    b Any rhyming word with **oo**, e.g. fool, drool, cool, school

    c Any rhyming word with **oo**, e.g. shoot, coot, boot, loot

10 a Any from: bike, by, buy, bite

    b Any from: high, hike, hide

    c Any from: lie, like, light, lime, lice

    d Any from: flight, fly

    e Any from: trike, trice, try, tribe, tripe

    f Any from: shy, shine

11 a I was go**ing** to school when I met a dog.

    b The lady show**ed** me the way to the park.

    c I have always want**ed** a hamster.

    d The fruit bat is fly**ing** in and out of the trees.

    e The scorpion dart**ed** towards the rocks.

    f The python is slither**ing** away.

12 a snappy   **b** funny

Well done, explorer!

You have finished your phonics and spelling adventure!

Explorer's pass

Name: _____

Age: _____

Date: _____

Draw a picture of yourself in the box!